The Quality of Mercy

James Clarke

HC
Press

Guelph, Ontario
2016

ISBN: (pbk) 978-1-928171-39-3
ISBN: (ebk) 978-1-928171-38-6

JHC
Press

Guelph, Ontario
2016

Reader – I tender these poems, scrimshaw on the walls of another dark cave, a reminder, should you find them, that the heart has its own reasons, and that we are, each in our own way a lone voyager, just passing through.

ACKNOWLEDGMENTS

I am indebted to my daughter Marilyn Clarke for the textile cover image, to my grandson James Clarke-Hicks for the emblem, to my daughter-in-law Carrie McClary for her editing, and to my friend Jeremy Luke Hill for the cover design and typesetting.

sun grows stronger, I
release the butterflies from
the net of my mind

The Quality of Mercy

James Clarke

THE PERFECT LOVELINESS OF NOW

THE HABIT OF MEMORY

opens skies within us,
a quickening of the heart forestalls
        the darkening of the mind, binds

mystery & mountains,
white flowers & wet sidewalks,
the scent of mildew & tea biscuits,
caws of crows and the shock of betrayal,
        old lovers and fading letters.

The hives of remembering rebuke the
        faceless & forgetful sun.

ANSWERED PRAYER

Even as winter comes &
days grow brief, I'm

grateful to be alive, awe-
struck & breathless

before the unceasing re-
birth of sun & great

blue promise of sky,
trusting in the Merciful

One who drew back the
curtain of darkness,

revealed the perfect
patience of mountains

amidst the wheeling stars.

VOYEUR OF THE NIGHT

I steal away to Palma's garden,
stroke the smooth skin of one of
her ripe tomatoes, taste its luscious
fruit. Dusk enfolds me, lightning
bugs appear, pulse with green light.
I go down to the shore, cast the cares
of the day into the marsh of memory,
become once more a voyeur of the
night, watch the stars undress.

SURVIVOR

Observe the dandelion. Study her habitat:
hanging pots, lawns, meadows, sidewalk
cracks & vacant lots. Purge your
conventional mind.

See how she lusts for light in all kinds of
weather, defies the grey death of asphalt
by thrusting her yellow head through
layers of paved convenience, the dank, leaden
earth. Note how the bees of summer sip her
wine. Let her wanton beauty twinge the heart,
dispel your inner dullness.

Impediments to progress are like that.

MILKWEED

Flicking open
                the dull green pod with
my fingernail
                my inner world is
startled alive
                by its hidden beauty –
a silky cone
                with serried ranks
of seedlings,
                nascent amber eyes.

Long after the silvery
                chutes floated out
of sight, the filaments
                still shimmer across
the dark insolvencies
                of my mind, –
a long-forgotten waterfall,
                a breath of pure light
whitening over rock..

GOLDFINCHES

The spring my friend lay dying
in the upstairs bedroom

of the old farmhouse we sat at
the kitchen table feeling

violated & annulled when suddenly
out of nowhere the

air was a dazzle of yellow brushstrokes
at the feeder, finches

chittering as though the first dawn
of creation had breathed

into being & they were birds
of imagination feasting

on a world that would never end.

CHECKHOV'S JOURNEY

On the Siberian Steppes on the last leg
of a journey of ten thousands versts, he
travelled in a contraption no bigger
than a cart, a tumbledown

Tarantass harnessed to two horses, drawn
by an old coachman, a "wicker basket"
he called it-twelve days of torture
over rutted roads, each jolt

a hammer in his back. As he observed
the passing milestones, puddles, birch
stands, the flat fields & log & sod huts
crowded with settlers, convicts, bums,

all the dumb & patient misery of humanity
sifted through his bones, cut like the cold
blade of wind that chafed his cheeks, pried
open his new leather overcoat; he saw

himself as a goldfinch in a cage peering
through bars at the harsh "once only"
in which we breathe & cast our shadow
a clear, unshuttered gaze, a God's eye,

seeing everything, forgetting nothing.

EL SALVADOR

"What's that?" I overheard the woman
on the tour bus ask her husband, pointing to
a steel sculpture looking like a bloated dart with
shark fins positioned on a concrete pad in a
schoolyard surrounded with flowers. "Oh,
that," he says, "it's a 500 lb bomb, the kind
the government dropped on civilians during
their scorched earth campaign against the
guerrillas, a memorial to the children blown
to pieces during the civil war. "Look," she
tells her husband, "those beautiful flowers,
I see them everywhere in this country. I wish
I knew their names."

CHANGE OF DIRECTION

Stripped down by age, the judge began to distance himself from his hectic courtroom life with its whirlpool of black words that sucked up so much light. He sought simple, neglected pleasures – listening in the shy light of morning as he sang in the bathroom, strolling in the city park to feed hungry pigeons or secluding himself in his garden to coax thoughts and poems out of hiding, enchanted by the faint, other-worldly sounds of birds and squirrels, the bell-notes of his once numinous existence.

EUCHARIST

I leave the courthouse
soiled & disillusioned, wander

down the aisle of the skin
care section of Shoppers

Drug Mart, seeking
that calamine of the soul –

Sunday morning last summer
when we sailed to the dayspring &

waves danced their liturgy for the risen
sun, three loons looked on

in meditation as a heron
prophesied from a driftwood stump &

poised above time, we forgot for
a few moments our

brokenness, slaked our thirst
in living water, shared bread

in our hearts.

ANGEL OF JUSTICE

Coaxing her to fly is never easy.
Mostly she's content to perch beside

me on the bench – a skinny angel
with wooden wings – play dumb

or press her eyelids closed, pretend
that she's asleep. Sometimes to get

her attention I tickle her dainty
feet or croon a ditty in her ear,

but she always feigns indifference,
lets on she doesn't hear or care.

Then just when you're tempted to put
her blindfold back & give her

up for dead she startles everyone
lawyers, litigants, reporters – all

the jaded crowd – by quickening back
to life, flaps her creaky hinges &

like the phoenix from the fire, soars
blueward in a blinding

rush of wings, higher & higher up
the corridors of air, till at last

she rings the halo of the sun.

STRAWBERRY PICKING
— for Palma

My eighty-two-year-old aunt
who claims she's beaten cancer

loves the earth so much she wants
to stay forever, taste

the sweetness of every waking day.
This afternoon as sun slanted

across a strawberry patch I watched
her stoop, a bent-over

child, to pick the heart-shaped fruit
stippled with yellow

seed, skin rougher than a cat's
tongue, break the globes of

red between her teeth, let
the juice dribble over her lip & chin,

one last time.

THE SMALL HEFT OF THE WORLD

One-by-one
      the black hooded singers came,
cautiously,
      then boldly,
a rush of wings,

swerving & swooping
      from branch to branch
to perch on our hands,
      tiny fishhook claws
clinging to the skin,

eating out of the
      hollow of our palms,
the small heft of the world,
      their warm beating bodies,
precious between our fingers.

NUNS

In October
> when twilight thickened
the air &
> candled eyes
of Jack-o-Lanterns
> gaped over dark hedges
we'd stop
> our game of chestnuts
long enough to watch
> them straggle out of school
black skirts billowing
> on the walkway,
their hands
> — white petals waving –
tourists from a far country.

DREAM OF THE LAST JUDGE

The spirit opens as life closes down.
— Jack Gilbert

Litigants stream out of the courthouse
into the spacious forecourt

of the heart, join hands, the green breath
of reconciliation on their lips.

Sun attends their every gesture; drop
by drop

ice melts into forgiveness, stones break
into flesh.

Spring hammers through earth, trees
burst into light.

GREAT BLUE HERON
— for Bruce

All day the hunter watched
as snow fell over lake and wood;
when sky emptied

its big, silk purse coins lay
scattered across the heavens;
and the hunter slept, dreaming

he was a great, blue heron. And while
he dreamt, three deer
stood on the snowy

lake gazing at the night;
and for a few moments the night held
handfuls of silver, the dreaming

hunter, and the three deer,
soft eyes impaled
by Orion's bright spears;

and when the hunter woke
only the windprints of the wings
remained.

A NEW BEGINNING

Leave the courthouse in the big city where you slog it out each day, sometimes deciding yes, sometimes no, discontent sizzling your blood.

Take the 401 all the way to Belleville, careful to avoid unnecessary stops and   detours, swing north onto highway 62 and continue on to Trudy's, the local store, where you always turn right. You're now on St. Ola road and not far from your destination. Eventually, make a sharp left turn onto Pleasure Bay Road and follow its winding bumpy course till you come upon a large A-frame with a green metallic roof. Now your heartbeat slows, the deadweight of law and worry lifts from your brow.

Go down to the lake, breathe the moist clean air and stand beneath the canopy of stars, listening till you begin to hear the sucking sound of gloom disappearing through a million white pinholes. Shed your city clothes, dive into the bracing waters. Stroke by stroke swim out into grace.

VAGARIES OF THE SPIRIT

COMPLINE

Coppery light fluttering

        on the cottage wall,

waves lapping

        on the shore;

summer & sunset

        & the long arms of contemplation

reach out to me

        as I write this poem,

recall your face,

        long to hear you say:

All, all is well,

        the sun – a crimson star

dying in my eyes.

WHAT THE BUDDHA TOLD ME

I came here to tell you certain things:
forget your fading map of cures; your
old life has not served you well. You
are something the wind caught standing
fast asleep & then moved on.

Listen, – the habitual sun fires up the sky;
the mottled world with all its radiant
voices longs to sing to you. Let me sit with
you awhile; we'll stay up all night, watch the
stars wheel by. In the morning I promise
you will wake.

WATCHING

others live their lives, watch your
    own life unfold.

Creatures of the universe –
    time's now to move on,
nudge yourself awake,
    trace the shift of the planets
for the alignment that
    lifts the heavy stone of fear.

We are not safe in the walled city
    under distempered skies.

Pray for that walk into grace, toward
    the blossoming sun.

ON BECOMING

Outside my window this New Year's
day, a winter storm. Vital parts of my
soul, captured by the storm, are snowed
under, dispersed with old dreams in the
whitened wind.

Some days I feel like a man carted off
in the gathering dusk, pushed into a wide
cold river with no name – a destiny no
New Year's resolution can change.

There can be no turning back, let the
clocks run late. I have outlasted fear, trust
my tired old body to take me each snowy
last step.

NIGHT EXECUTION

The darkness around me is deep
as I listen to him scrabbling

in the wall, nuzzling
for crumbs or a nest to rest

his head. I find it hard to
ignore his presence, get some

sleep, but when I hear the jaws
snap shut, the scraping on

the floor, I spring awake, switch
on the lamp, remove the panel

behind the door, beam my flash-
light in. The trap (two for one

at the DOLLAR Store) is
tilted on its side, the brass bar

that promised instant death
missed the neck, fell across

the spine instead. I pull on yellow
rubber gloves, reach inside and

bring him out, alive – a rag toy –
crushed in two with

big imploring eyes; I hesitate,
but only for a second

– his back is broken, he cannot
live. I must do what I must do,

then rush to wash my hands
and back to sleep.

SARTORI IN SURIN

The old monk led me
into the inner courtyard;
above us perched the

Buddha on his lacquered
dais – a golden pear.
Doves burbled on the

ivied walls, fragrance
of jasmine filled the air, a
breeze ruffled the skin

of the pool. The old monk
clasped my hand; the pool
rilled with tiny suns;

I thought I heard the tinkle
of bells from far away. There
was a breath of wings, a

tremble of light as though
a dark bird had flown
from my brow. Something

happened; I do not know.

JUDGE'S PRAYER

What pardon for this, Lord?
All my life I pursued Reasonable Doubt,
clung to her like a drowning sailor
to a raft at sea,
did not always follow your command
to smite the wicked,
                    set the innocent free.

I doubted, Lord, & I doubted, Lord, till
my mind grew grey. Forgot your way Lord.
More than your certitudes, Lord, I loved
the shifting shape of reason-
its enthrallments & futilities, shovelled
clouds of words into the wide mouth of doubt,
                    eschewed prejudice & sympathy
danced like a besotted lover
on the cool blue pinhead of logic
till the legs within my legs gave out, all
passion spent.

What pardon for this, Lord: Just lawgiver, Harbour and
Master?
I plead guilty, deserve
to be punished.

A CERTAIN IMAGE

haunts the judge's dreams.
Standing over a deep well
he grips the ankles of the guilty
and before he lets go
glimpses terror
on their faces.
Then, pity ticking in his ear,
he leans his head
into the rounded darkness,
listening
for the splash.

THE SWEET LONGING

The old judge lifted the garlic jar to the light,
jade-coloured, ringed like Saturn, ash deposits
on its fire face, a circlet of five air holes near
the base. The potter's note said it was ripened
in a river of fire – a two-chambered "Japanese
style" climbing kiln – wood stoked for twenty
hours – a plain but elegant artifact, glazed with
love to adorn someone's kitchen for years.

Leaving the studio he felt strangely downcast
thinking about all the time he'd spent
peering down the fractious throats of Right &
Wrong looking for guilt or innocence, always
deciding yes or no, waking most days from
a dream-tossed sleep, the first rays of pale sun
poking through dusty glass, never knowing
if he'd ever created anything that lasts.

SENTENCING

I wonder
if people like Billy – the big,
swarthy man with burning eyes
who appears before me
PROUD TO BE MOHAWK stamped on his sweat
shirt – will ever cease to be a displaced
person;

I remember when
men like Billy stole into town
Saturday mornings to peddle
pickerel and mudcat
door to door
for extra dimes,
their breath reeking of rye and
respectable moms and dads called
them drunken Indians
and
children mocked them with war cries
just like in the cowboy movies.

It's true
that Billy's parents were both alcoholics,
that his dad abandoned them when he was
five,
that he can barely read or write,
that he drinks too much for his own good,
that he carries a log on his
shoulder,

but all the sensitivity training in the world
won't help Billy today,
who crossed the centre line and smashed
another car, putting the driver in
hospital with a broken leg,
now convicted for the fourth time
of impaired driving;
"I have no choice, but to send
you to jail for a long time," I say.

But deterrence is only white
man's mumbo jumbo to Billy,
so I quickly do what I have to do
and leave,
wondering if Billy thinks he's being screwed again
by white man's justice.

In the hallway my constable smirks:
"That was one surprised Indian."
I glare at his smug, white face,
until I see myself
reflected back.

THE WAY OF THE PROPHET

Your heart's a crib of thorns, but
Then they pluck them one by one &

Blood pours out, a sticky lake, in
Which you nearly drown, your body

Redder than a cardinal's rib cage.
Now you know you're on the way, but

First the grind of bone & socket, a hail
Of spit & stones, the clown in stripes

Who mops your brow. And then before
You reach the grisly spot you see the

Judge draped in silk, the surly soldiers
Drawing lots. You scarcely feel the

Pain slip in before they pin you to the
Tree. And the sharp surmise

Rising in your eyes that maybe you have
Failed, that all your strivings were

In vain, pierces the darkening like a nail.

BIRTHDAY PARTY

After the boys stopped fighting
— you must learn to get along
with one another –
the parents chided,

the mother of the birthday boy
reminded him that it was polite
to always open the cards
first, and never forget
to say thank you. Meanwhile

on the coffee table
the gifts: plastic dagger,
cosmic ray gun, Risk-
world conquest game,
Karate-fighters, "the real
hand-to-hand" combat kit,
box of toy soldiers, etc.,

kept piling up, small mines,
the kind that blow off toes
or hands, blind the eye.

THE FUNHOUSE

In this funhouse, ringed with mirrors,
fantasy holds full sway, dreams have their
way with you. Everyone floats free, plays
at hide-and-seek. Wherever you look you
can never find yourself & creatures in
grotesque disguises – clown with angel
wings, toothless monkey, greying, grumpy
judge – shout & ask – who are you? but nobody
answers. Here no one knows their name till
their last breath gives out.

PALM-IN-THE-HAND STORY

One evening a gang of murderers & thieves
came to the monastery at Assisi seeking
food & lodging-Francis was away, preaching
in a nearby village. When Brother Antonio

unbolted the door & observed their unsavoury looks,
he panicked, told them the monastery was full. After
Francis returned next day & learned what
had happened he called his followers together.

"Everyone's our brother & sister," he told them.
Then he instructed Antonio to find the outcasts
& bring them back to the monastery so they could
make amends. When Antonio found the gang

camped in a field not far from the monastery he
was filled with remorse. He knelt on the ground
before them, bowed his head & begged for
forgiveness. In one clean blunt stroke his head

went flying through the air like an ear of corn.
The gang stripped his tunic, left his naked body
in the field & sent his severed head back to the
monastery in a stolen oxcart. When Francis saw

the beatific look on Antonio's face, he lifted eyes
to heaven in thanksgiving, praised God for
his infinite mercies.

HOLY THURSDAY

In the Egypt of Landlord and Tenant court
at Brampton this Holy Thursday,
where a throng from
all races, creeds, and walks of life
murmurs in the rotunda:
tenants who can't pay rent,
landlords who can't pay mortgages,
unemployed fathers,
single welfare moms,
the mentally afflicted,
the physically disabled,
scoundrels, saints, everyone

lugging a sack of bad luck:
no money, no job, Powers of Sale, leaky
roofs, faulty furnaces, flooded basements,
dripping faucets, attic squirrels,
sudden sickness, government treachery,
hungry children,
runaway husbands (etc.),

there are no tambourines
of thanksgiving,
just the rough deliverance
of the law,
with no paschal blood
on the door posts
to guide my slippery sword.

KAFKA'S PARABLES

What are you to do? asks Kafka. When he says "go over" to this place, he's not talking about Jerusalem on the hill, some actual place, but the "fabulous yonder" of the unknown, the incomprehensible. My friend Jim, the professor who teaches Kafka's parables, says that when you let parables stew in your mind, it's difficult to refocus on the everyday. But don't be tricked, Kafka would say, some go blind trying to understand the unsolvable, unlock the "why." What I say is this: let your struggle with daily cares vanish in the smoke of heaven. Become your own parable – accept the mystery.

A QUEER BEAST
— a fable

A man thought he was a dog & started walking on all fours. He lost his elegant manners, panted & drooled at the sight of food & bayed furiously in the middle of the night. Occasionally he'd snap at passers-by. Most of the time he'd slouch through fields with rainwater eyes, hunker down in tall weeds & yip in his sleep.

One day someone told him he was made in the image of God. The news hit like a blizzard of light. He immediately set about abandoning his feral ways, learned to walk upright & tried to take on his true Godshape.

But old habits die hard. Nowadays you can find him most evenings honing his teeth in dark alleyways, the old lust for murder & mayhem still gleaming in his eyes.

A STORY FOR A LIFE

The squirrels in my yard have no problem with identity; every day they leap from branch to branch, skirmishing with kith & kin oblivious of greed & grief, doing what comes naturally in their DNA-coded lives. Unlike the squirrels, I have been thrust willy-nilly into the world, fitted for a role that left me trying to figure out how to escape the steely script of destiny, find the courageous wisdom to chose the one story that is mine alone to live.

A CERTAIN JUDGE

considers himself a man of logic. He dismisses the concept of right & left hemispheres of the brain as another example of junk science. In his highly partisan view of his experience, emotion & imagination are a menace, bits of foreign grit in the smooth functioning of the law; poets & artists, a burden on the workaday world. "Logic is the true religion," he tells himself. The lawyers who encounter his single-track thinking, know him as the judge with half a brain.

A POET'S WORK

Just as a bird twig by twig builds a nest on
some precarious limb to outlast cruel winds,
so I, in these latter days, labour in spin-drift
light, poem by poem, to fend off grief, hoping
what I love will last.

MORNING RESOLUTION

I arise, shower, breakfast, avow my good intentions,
leave for court to deal with a custody battle with two
vociferous and truculent lawyers who despise one
another with a passion. On the way to the courthouse I
turn on the car radio, listen to the latest play-by-play
description of human misery and remind myself that
being a judge is not, if one listens to the news, the worst
fate that can befall a person on this troubled earth.

THE TENDER GRAVITY OF KINDNESS

INTERCESSION

Forsake me not, Lord,
       hold me near, teach
me I have nothing to fear.
       Though only lightly
here I will not break:
       I was not lightly made.

THE LAST CARAVAN TO DAMASCUS
— for Gay & Graham

A singularly bleak December it was,
cold, icy, our bodies flaring in the winter
moonlight; we cut a deal with the police,

but planned a different route; we all knew
the importance of a good story. Marauding
bands of zealots almost did us in, forced us

to detour around their camps. When I dropped
out at the Temple to buy bagels and a teddy
bear the others went ahead with the baskets

of gifts; I scrambled to catch up but never
saw them again. No star shone in the darkness;
no sleigh bells jingled in

the air. The evening turned out more bodiless
than I ever dared imagine. By the time
I found the hostel—a rude and drafty barn, shocked

to see the Press already there—the family had
fled, vanished beasts and all without a trace, no
forwarding address. I was disappointed to say

the least; missed connections are the story
of my life. Humiliated too; the shepherds
snickered behind my back. I gave the bagels and

teddy bear to street kids, what else to do?
left that hostile land as ceremoniously as I could,
caught the last caravan to Damascus.

But despite my disappointment a voice
inside my heart kept whispering not to fret,
the family was happy and unharmed. Now

years later, many bizarre and terrible things
have come to pass—too numerous to relate;
but when I think of that freezing barn

I still regret I came too late, never
saw the child, feel a twinge of pity for
the young man who was me, a callow

adventurer in a strange country, benighted and
alone without a map, no one to thank,
no gifts to unwrap.

SOMETIMES I FEEL PITY

for the not-so-good thief,
you know, the one who leaves finely sculpted
footprints in snowdrifts and perfect fingerprints
on fridge doors, florid calling cards;
the hapless creature
who, nabbed red-handed with the smoldering goods
in the back of the open pickup,
is struck speechless until
at the station
he opens his heart to the first officer
who promises to be his friend, sealing the alliance
with a signed inculpatory statement;
yes, there has to be a place
in paradise even for the clumsy thief,
whose simplicity
makes us want to forgive,
like Jesus,
his artless mischief.

UNEXPECTED GIFT

After dismissing the sexual
assault charge because the Crown
had failed to prove its case
beyond a reasonable doubt

the judge observed the accused,
a free man now, smirk
he shook the hand
of counsel.

Entering his chambers,
the judge met the interrogating
eyes of his five daughters on
his desk (how can you ever

explain that probable guilt
is never enough?)
and his spirit began to sink
in the spongy bog

of an imperfect justice system,
till he heard someone
outside his window
in the April sunshine, whistling,

the kind of tuneless
whistling you do when Spring
unfurls its new flags, trembles
with green mercy.

INFLATION

Once upon a time
        a judge lost his
steely, fevered grip
        on rationality,
morphed into
        a transgressive
in the eyes of his
        fellow travelers.
Lawyers quaked,
        litigants trembled
& justice wobbled
        before the broadside
of his deviant opinions.
        Only heretics took
heart, their long-suffering
        faces brightening
at the prospect of a
        new dispensation.

WISHFUL THINKING

What if judges had the gift to set free the power of
words like "forgiveness," "reconciliation" and
"peace"?

What if all it took was to direct arguments so that
everyone could taste again the ancient honey of this
healing language?

How beautiful it would be to watch old habits melt
away, see litigants and lawyers roll the syllables on
their tongues, shed their reptilian brain and rise
reasonable and sane?

What if "love" were such a word?

"Shalom" I would say.

WINTER SOLSTICE

I grieve the cold, trackless
stars, the shadows, sharply

bent and harsh against the snow;
wind in trees outside my window

moves like someone passing. Moon
is full—a large pearly bulge; no

telescope can explain its cool
back-lit glow; the earth

tilts on its axis, flies elliptically
around the sun but even

on darkest days the sun stands
still; it is we who leave.

The lamp in my kitchen is not
strong enough to

pierce the dark, the weight of
absence presses against

the glass. I've decided to
burn a candle, however

brief, await the slow unfettered
light of dawn, let

memory sweeten grief.

INVISIBLE COMMUNION

Life is a dance and dance is life.
                    — Martha Graham

When his young colleague at the judge's conference
leaned over & whispered "What do those two old
crocks still see in each other?" nodding discreetly toward
an elderly white-haired couple at the next table eating
in silence as though they had nothing more to say to
one another,

what the older man couldn't tell him (& what perhaps he might
never see) was the invisible tango being enacted before
their eyes, the slow mute dance of two old lovers gentling
into forgiveness.

CONSOLATION
— inspired by Wislawa Szymborska

The old gods, often preoccupied
and fickle, sometimes perverse,
are neither gullible nor indifferent.
They know that we all must die,
understand our deep, consuming
fears. The old gods are not as heart-
less as we deign to think. They can,
on occasion, see our sadness and
take pity, toss a dead loved one into
our dreams.

LOST FEATHER

Remember that August morning at the lake,
the sparrow on the deck knocked silly
by the window pane,
a brown fluff
unable to fly or walk,

how the children found the shoe box,
tore up strips of newspaper for a bed,
and you, who always taught
Jesus never forgets his smallest ones,
placed the lost feather at its side;
"Every feather counted," you said.

Then loyal to family lore
you fed the bird a drop of whisky.
"He'll fly again."

And next morning the sparrow
had raised his bones and fled,
resurrected.

Then what went wrong my darling wife
that Palm Sunday afternoon?
Did He not offer you a drop
before you fell?

ACCEPT THE BLESSING

You walk in an orchard in spring
bloom, worried about tomorrow. The
limbs of the apple trees hang low. Pink
blossoms whisper: *breath this air, let
the future go. Afraid?* Accept the gifts
that fall your way.

HIDDEN DEVOTIONS

Those cold-knuckled dark winter mornings
in the tenement during the war, he'd lay
upstairs-awake – listening to his mother
in the kitchen stacking the grate, raking
the ash pan to capture the dying sparks,
lingering in his feather-down bed until
stars winked out & the white fan of dawn
appeared. How little he knew in those un-
fledged years of the costly, unsung labours
of love.

ENVOI

Unglove your hand –
     hidden in this cage
of cells is the lifebird;
     set free what waits
to call your name, help you
     forget the night's frost,
break open your cold,
     stony heart.

TENEBRAE

A crisp May morning of shell-ice
puddles & brittle grass. At the Golden
Teaspoon the owner extols the virtues
of his hot chocolate.

I scan the book section of
the Globe, a line from Dante incised
on the gravestone of Primo Levi catches
my eye: "Consider your seed; you were

not made to live like brutes." Strolling
through the Farmer's Market, I drop
a coin into the blue of the fiddler's violin case,

and I wish I could shed my impediments,
but memory defines me. Soon, I know,
a summer of leafing voices will be here,

then the long fields tawny with stubble
& the Day of the Dead, & once more
lost names shall inhabit the darkening air,

their dry dimly-remembered
conversations whispering in my head.

PRAYER FOR JUSTICE

Bring the clear mirror,
let her see
the jaded eye,
the unforgiving mouth,
let her face break down in tears.

Give back her brown nakedness,
her four, strong limbs,
let her breathe freely,
break softly into new fields.

GRAMMAR OF COMPLICITY

Enhanced interrogation, not water-boarding,
collateral damage, not killing of innocents,
an evil empire, never opposition.

A word-heap of deceit, just enough to veil
the truth, dampen our anxiety, pacify the
conscience.

In a less-confused time, seeing ourselves from
a distant, wider horizon, the ardour for war
faded, we will see more clearly, learn why
we were so terrified, and what happened here.

RUSH TO JUDGMENT

The Hell's Angel with
locks the colour of dandelions,
pink muscle T-shirt & gold earrings – a blue
skeleton on a motorcycle, RIDE HARD,
DIE FREE tattooed on his right
bicep – shambled to the witness
box & testified
how he saw the blue Cutlass skid
into the concrete
abutment, stopped his bike &
stayed with the woman whose legs were jammed
under the steering column,
stroking her
hand, whispering to her like a lover &
lost his job as bouncer
at the Brass Rail all-day
strip club for being late.

THE QUALITY OF MERCY

With a comic book robber's mask he glides
along the veranda ledge & stops, pushes his

sharp snout through a slit in the screen &
in one motion of liquid grace, nips

inside. "She's my regular guest," says Palma,
reaching inside a pail to scatter a fistful

of minnows on the floor. "I feed her every
day." The raccoon rears, ringtail curled

& flared, long fluid fingers & sharp,
curving claws poised in mid-air. The

tiny dark fish leap & wiggle-wag on
the linoleum, gasping for deliverance. "Last

week my neighbours shot her four babies," she
says, "they warned me not to be so kind."

GODFINDER
— *i.m. Etty Hillesum*

In Westerbork the doctor, furious, said:
"Why are you smiling, it's unforgivable
to smile in times like this."

When an old woman asked: "Could you
tell me please, why we Jews suffer
so much?" she couldn't answer.

Sometimes she berated herself for being a
dreamer, not having her feet on the ground.
Though she knew Jews had reason

to hate she chose a different path: believed
the earth could only be made habitable
again through love.

Amidst the routine terror of the wooden
barracks she prayed that she might become
a balm for all wounds.

Saving our bodies was not what matters,
she wrote, but how we preserve them.
All day she dressed babies,

calmed mothers, helped to carry baggage
for the transport to "to the East." That evening
as sun set on the heath she observed

through the barbed wire a guard, an enraptured
look on his face, rifle dangling, stoop
to pick a bouquet of purple lupins.

HOW TO BUILD A MODERN BIRD HOUSE

Decide what species you want.
Measure the entrance
with care; neither big enough

for predators nor small enough
to ruffle feathers. Assemble
your tools: handsaw, claw hammer,

screwdriver & drill.
Keep the saw well honed,
cut with a steady eye.

Make slits for drainage &
ventilation; a bird should feel
part of earth & sky

not a prisoner in his own
castle. Finally, hang the
birdhouse near shrubs &

trees, where birds like to
nest. Remember, a house
cobbled together

cannot last. Hammer
love between your nails.

IF AMELIA STARTS TO CRY
— found poem

put her in her blue snuggly; don't sit down
or relax, otherwise she won't stop.

Check her diaper, leave if not too damp.
If she's wearing a disposable

that's not too dirty, don't attempt a change
as this will upset her more. Remember

she can't feel the pee-pee on her bum if it's
a disposable. Pat her forehead (not too hard)

to see if she's cool. Put her in her cosy
nighttime clothes if necessary. Or feed her

some rice cereal mixed with water and banana
(a third) from her Peter Rabbit cup.

And don't forget her special spoon. Hold her
standing up, rocking back and forth as though

dancing. Dance until she calms. Put her
on your lap and play peek-a-boo or kiss her

cheeks rhythmically. Or give her a toy, care-
ful not to overstimulate her – such a fine

balance. If she continues to cry console her
as soon as possible, put her in the pram,

move it back and forth in the front hall or
if she co-operates take her for a walk

around the block. Or put her in the carseat
and take her for a short drive. Sometimes

she wants your full attention – nothing
less will do.

Sing – she won't know if you have no voice –
sing, sing, sing.

THE ACHE OF ABSENCE

LACRIMAE RERUM

This morning Rosie's heart knotted
in pain: her beautiful pink balloon
burst in mid-air, suddenly vanished &
she doesn't know why.

Child, dry your tears fast; though
now you can't guess, more grief's
to come – pink balloon's the first,
but won't be the last.

DARK NIGHT OF THE SOUL

Love is not consolation, it is light.
           – Simone Weil

Days pass when we forget the mystery –
stars that once whispered of infinite light
retreat into unfathomable dark, indifferent
to our fate.

Have mercy on us, Lord – bereft seekers
who no longer hear the quiet call
of lost heavens.

HER LAST GIFT

"Remember," she said in the hospital
when the black dog howled in her mind,
"you've been a good husband and
a good father, never forget it."

She was preparing for the hour
when he would stand before their children,
mouth stopped with grief,
heart swollen, the "ifs"
twisting like a dull blade.

"I forgive you husband, father
and when you look
into the beautiful dark water of my death
forgive me too, and learn to love
the face you see."

PÉPÈRE

i

Sometimes in the night
I'd hear him groan
on the iron cot under the stairway,
the slap of mom's bare feet
on the linoleum as
she hurried to fetch pills
from the kitchen
or change soiled sheets,
        soft voice
talking to him in French
like a baby.

ii

One morning – in the before dawn dark –
she shook me awake:
" Pépère's sick," she told me
racing breathless ten blocks
through rain in my new
white running shoes, pounding
on Dr. O'Brien's door
till his face appeared, a sleepy
apparition behind curtains;
"Quick, quick, Pépère's sick."

iii

I want to die "dans mon pays,"
he said.

iv

I lean against the yellow hydrant
in front of the tenement,
as mom, teary-eyed,
          bundles him
into the back seat
of Mr. Colson's green '39 Ford
for the long trip home,
glimpse him for the last time:
wrapped in a blue blanket,
battered brown fedora
jammed on his head
sucking his pipe.

v

Mom and my aunt
sip brandy at the kitchen table
– remembering
while I listen –
mom mumbling over and over:
"His time had come" as though words had
power to reconcile,
          learning
how we are all joined together,
how love can only be broken
one link at a time.

VANITY OF HUMAN WISHES

Poets have always drawn language
        from the shadows within themselves,
turned houseflies into gold.
        "Never waste good agony,"
grandmother used to say.
        Beatrice Hawley, who loved Rilke,
saw poetry a means of redeeming time,
        a "particularly happy & pure way
of living." She made
        an unswerving commitment
to create a few good poems,
        give them some amulet
they could wear "as they try, like
        little birds, to fly in the world
apart from me."

But even the dark bread of
        her poems couldn't save her,
the cancer reached up &
        pulled her down &
she forgot the shape
        little birds make in the air.

AT THE FUNERAL HOME

I arrive early, wait in the vestibule.
"Funerals let us say goodbye" reads
in the message in the pale-gold frame
above the reception desk. The Director
ushers me into a room with washed-
out light, the smell of furniture polish.

You're laid out on a gurney in your
good blue pin-striped suit, your mouth
clamped shut, all your well-mapped
lines of living expunged from brow &
cheeks. I listen for the rise & fall of a
single breath. What I hear is stillness &
silence in this dark parlour stuffed with
loss. "*Forgive me brother,*" I whisper
as I rise to leave. "*I'm not yet ready
today to say goodbye.*"

THE DENSITY OF GRIEF

I observe my old neighbour trudging home past my house clutching his coat collar on this cold, blustery January evening. I've only spoken to him once – a casual encounter years ago when we first moved into town. Distraught, he urgently wanted to talk about his brilliant young daughter, a medical graduate, and her recent death at 28 from a brain tumour. Still stunned by the hammer blow of my first wife's suicide – I later wondered whether it was our common bereavement that made him think he wanted to talk with me – I was barely able to respond. Now twenty years later my failure to reach out & touch his pain still preys on my conscience. Strangers we remain, wrapped in our separate grief, passing under white trees, almost invisible in the snowy night.

FLUX

Under the melting snow
a red tricycle takes shape,

apple blossoms, lighter
than the blue silk sky,

stream before your eyes;
seasons come & go,

but no matter how gently
I touch the rose the petals

will fall, the soft circle
round the fire will break &

leaf by leaf the darkening
trees grow cold;

the long goodbyes never
seem to cease, nothing

stays the same or whole.

THE ACHE OF ABSENCE

Always a departing
        train, a last wave &
the receding station,

dust devils & swirl-
        ing roadside trash,
the face of some-

one you love
        there one moment,
then gone –

waking in a house
        of viewless light
unable to breathe.

REMEMBRANCE OF THINGS PAST

We climbed to the top of the bluff – our
old picnic grounds, that balmy October
afternoon. "*The hills of heaven wait,*"
you said. How could we know
then that within a year you would cross the
chalk line between being here & being else-
where. Now all I remember of that early fall
day is the blue dome of cloudless sky & how
light the world felt in my arms.

UNDYING HOPE

In old black and white photos,
in the steely mirror of cold skies,
on the glassy walls of malls,
in my nightly dreams & the glowing
eyes of our children you trail behind
my shadow, briefly show yourself.

Every spring I hope to see
you rise triumphant with the trilliums,
but when I try to hold your image,
memory betrays me & slides away.
Where do you go? And where have
you been hiding?

WHAT THE JUDGE FAILED TO MENTION

In sentencing the young man to prison the judge told him: "I hope you have learned that crime does not pay." What the judge failed to mention were all the other lessons the young man would learn in that under-world of stone where everyone is allotted a wedge of unreachable sky & redemption is in short supply, where love belongs to a lost language & everyone drinks from the same wormwood cup, where you wake each morning in a sunless cell too small for dreams, left to wonder where the light of the world has fled.

A LATE NIGHT PRAYER

After he found the two men guilty
they'd picked up the young woman
in a bar on Jarvis Street, driven her to a field
north of the city, beaten & raped her,
then, slitting her throat with a hunting knife,
left her for dead –

the judge went home that evening
steeped in gloom, listened to the evening
news, another chronicle of blighted hopes,
convinced humanity had fallen off a moral cliff,
sought solace in his garden to gaze
        at the shimmering roof of stars,
the full moon, its radiance
        borrowed from the sun,

startled to find himself, talking to the night,
something he'd never done before,
        his fist clenched, shouting:
"How long, God, do we have to wait before
 you change our blood-bent ways?"

THE QUARRY
— for Monsignor Newstead

I'm a trader, not a philosopher. I pay
my taxes, keep my camels fed;
religion does not engage my better self
or interest me.

Not that I have much faith in the goat
of humanity. Once in Damascus
I witnessed the police chop off the hand
of a boy for stealing figs. In the passes

I've come across brigands lashed to rocks,
left for the vulture's meal. I've learned it's
best to look the other way, keep the lips
sealed. What then made me stop?

I heard the shouts, glimpsed the woman
kneeling in the dust, the upraised stones
like fists of gold; I saw him step
forward, talk to them,

then write with finger on the ground.
One by one, starting with the elders,
they threw down their stones, drifted off,
till there was no one left but me.

Afterward, I searched the earth for clues.
Nothing, nothing at all, just whorls of
sand and bits of broken rock. Now I'm only
a businessman, but no fool; in the cold

light of justice I know all of us would
come up short. Some say he was a sorcerer
and cast a spell. Did he give them
back their guilt? My wife complains I'm too

curious for my own good, that I shouldn't meddle
 in matters beyond my ken. Small
wonder I toss and turn at night, she harps.
And yet, how can I forget:

the fire in the woman's eyes, the quarry
stones burning in the sun?

PROPER BURIAL

We must give them a proper burial
the poet from Jamaica said
of the 25,000 slaves
destined for the islands
pitched into a watery grave.

O how we tried to give you a proper burial
that sunny afternoon in Easter week,
while your portrait gazed at us
from the sanctuary,

sprinkling you with holy water,
robing you with incense,
singing till we could no longer hear
your unquiet spirit. And still

at Eastertide I sometimes hear
lilies weeping in the sun, your voice
like Niagara, roaring in the night.

REVENANT

Woke up suddenly – a nightshift
of crickets outside our bedroom
window, thinking
– only for the briefest second –
you were there beside me on the bed &
I could breathe your breath in the blue night
air, deeply, slowly,

reached across the sheets to touch
your cheek – stopped, remembered;
the moonlight on your pillow cold.

SUMMER MELANCHOLY

6 a.m. at the lake &
already I'm awake, wrapped

in expectation; across
the bay a loon calls;

daylight faint & feathery
as breath

riffles curtains, birds
open their eyelids,

unfold their wings, begin
to sing,

but this plentitude
is deceiving:

soon autumn will be here &
cold will touch

the lake, a black pane
chipped with stars,

to smoky glass & then
to white;

in the spring snow
& ice will disappear &

small green buds with
forked tails

will swim like fishes
in the blue, bees

fumble in the Indian
Paintbrush by the shore,

but I'll still be hushed &
sad, thinking

of you & how I should
have held you

in my arms, closed your
eyes with kisses.

OF THE DEAD

I remember you, hold you close.
When all the bells of heaven are
quiet, your name tolls in my dreams.
Your face peers through my candled
windows asking questions that I do
not know how to answer.

Here, absence shouts loud, leaves
an emptiness. Wind bends the yellow
wheat. Death drops its torn glove on
our paths. Nothing remains steadfast,
only the cold stars do not blow way.

LET MORNING COME

DELIVERANCE

Haunted by
    old regrets,
I traverse the burnt
    ground of memory,
praying for
an end to darkness.

Fully awake now,
    light creeps back,
leaves catch the sun,
owls return
    to nest,

the dark night retreats,
my prayers answered.

THE ROAD HOME

Temporary detour. The court is inundated
with pages of acrimony and falsehood. The
promise of justice lies in a crumpled heap. A
scent of desperation taints the air.

Come evening, I will leave the scene, make
my way home, remind myself that it is not my
destiny to cure the ills of a distempered human
ity. To the brief reprieve of sleep, I'll yield,
close my lids like stones, patiently
await the appearance of a new day.

MATINAL

Groggy from sleep
        I rub my lids;
a sickle moon pins
        the fraying shirt
of night; across
        the bay a frog
trumpets the end
        of dark. Soon
bands of
        pink and white
will span the sky,
        ream the runneled
bark, ignite
        a pathway for
the sun.

Night is done –
        so much to rue,
so much to do;
        let morning come.

RELUCTANT JOURNEY
 — *after Jack Gilbert*

Knowing he had no choice,
     he lifted the unwieldy stone
into his awkward arms,
     walked across the endless
fields, shifting its weight
     from time to time to ease
the pain, often stopping
     to lay it down, catch his
breath, before taking it
     up again, befriended his
burden mile after mile till
     it became the weightless
ballast of his wounded life.

REDEMPTION

We leave home to save ourselves. Resisting inertia, we allow life to rush in, erase limits of imaginary boundaries that confine us, walk alien lands under star-dusted skies, no place to rest. One day we waken. Haunted by old ghosts, we feel the weight of memory – the slanted roof, iron latch, musty smells, a throng of forgotten loves beckoning us home, where the gravity of the world is lifted, back to the shining, white stone bearing our name.

THE WAY EVERYONE IS INSIDE

What are you doing with your life?
This is a good Buddhist question.
You didn't buy it.
It's quite sobering, but the way
the world is being organized, bigger parts
of it are sliding inexorably into
smaller, where we live,
we don't even know we're being bruised.

When the raging elephant (or angry
boss, it makes no difference) comes charging
it's already too late.

The old millennium is darkening like a window,
the bus is breaking down:
ball bearings have sprung loose, we're desperately
in need of a cosmic catching mitt – a fresh way
of seeing;
a new sun's begging to be born.

THE BEARDED LADY Of POETRY

When you encounter the bearded lady in the schoolyard
refuse to act like the schoolmarm, ruffled lace at her neck,
copper ruler in hand who demands an explanation. Don't
forbid her to leave the schoolyard or even worst send her
to the stern principal for correction. The bearded lady is
not computable; wants to be herself, a mystery to be reveal-
ed. Stand back and respect her for who she is . She desires
not just your intellect but your whole crystallized self –
nerve endings, dreams, images, all five senses, memory – ,
what exists alive (though sometimes dozing) in you that you
don't know how to say. If you're lucky & patient & curious
she may in her own good time tell you her secrets , shape
your understanding in ways you could never have guessed.
Watch how she moves; the bearded lady is a wanderer.
Once outside the yard she'll slip away anywhere, anytime.
And if you're ready she'll beckon you to come along, let you
follow her footprints into the snow-white light.

LISTEN FRIEND

I write these poems
for you who whisper
why.

Am I just to think I'm
a stuffed seabird,
tweeting to myself,
my wingless breath
grayer than pebbles
on a deserted shore?

Take these words, I say,
toss them skyward, watch
them catch the sun,
rekindle once more
that fire on your tongue.

IF YOU WANT TO BE STRUCK BY LIGHTNING

You mustn't be afraid
– trees; planets, seas, know nothing else –
learn to feel the first faint kiss of wind,
the fleck of rain on skin &
leaving all behind forsake the shadows
where you've cowered all these years
for the high ridge above the timberline or better yet,
a wide pond where you can stand &
stretch your naked arms,
embrace the thundery sky & wait.

And after you've been zapped right through,
your head uncapped, your heart electric blue,
pretend that you are dying, refuse
cardiac compression,
all mouth-to-mouth resuscitation &

when they've finally given you up for dead & left,
take up your life again with simple breath,
        unpeel the inner eye,
see the silver & blue insects thrumming round your head,
the blossoming pear tree struck to light

SPRING THAW

It has been
a long, hard winter.
The iron lake
is still dreaming

the rumble
of unpacking snow,
the whips
of cracking ice,
trickling water
in the sun.

Silver eyes
open blueward.
The lake is waking up,
elephants are walking.

YOU ARE MY BELOVED
— for Bobby

Buried deep in the unfathomable heart
surrounded by darkness, the seed finds
a stony place. Patiently we moisten its
tiny roots with life-giving water, make an
airy space for it to breathe and grow.
This can go on for a long time, till we
wonder if green shoots will ever come.
Then one morning we wake from troubled
sleep to find the hard earth broken and
surprise: – an amaryllis blooming before
our awestruck eyes, a voice whispering,
I am Love and you are my beloved.

THE MINGLING

That spring morning after Benoit,
one of the young residents at L'Arche,
choked to death in his sleep
(he'd had an epileptic seizure)
I met Pere Thomas, swishing
to chapel along the Rue Principale
clad in his long, loose Dominican
habit, the pale sun shining
on his pate. "Too bad about Benoit,"
I said. He glanced at me kindly,
lifted his pale blue eyes
to the sky & said, almost as if I'd
missed the point: "Benoit
is now with the Father in Heaven."
Then he smiled & added:
"Death's our real birthday."

A short time after your death
when I told a visiting priest
from Sri Lanka that you'd leapt
to your drowning at Niagara,
he said, eyes suddenly aglow:
"Wow, imagine being swept
into the arms of Jesus, it takes
my breath away." His voice rose
as he urged me to make a retreat
at the Carmelite monastery.

"Let your prayers mingle
with the mighty waters," he said.

A PECULIAR BEAUTY

In the seamy parts of the bloated city
the maze of avenues confuse with pleasure;

amidst the ghostly highrises trucks growl,
cruise the streets past dogs, cats, sparrows.

Geraniums crowd cracked stoops & rusty
fire escapes. In the subway station a young

couple hug & kiss, a woman drops a coin
in the hat of the man on his knees. A wino

in the park basks in the sun, watches the
old ballerina walk her cat on a leash.

Beware crass prophets of gloom who sniff
the air, celebrate death, declare all we need

for the good life are pockets of power, mouth
fuls of gold. Assassins of light, their oracles

darken the mind & flatten the earth, doom
us to wither like unwatered grass.

THE LAST WISHLIST

After the reading the young poet approached the judge with a question: "Why did you become a poet?" The judge, who had taken up poetry after his wife's death, had routinely answered that question many times before, but on this occasion, his words crumbled in his mouth.

The young poet would have unaccounted years ahead to test the slopes of love, write her poems, compile her own list of squandered affections, taste the wormwood of failed dreams. When the judge was young he thought growing old a quaint illusion. Now his unfinished wishlist began to unscroll in his head: keep evil at bay, disarm sharp tongues, dampen the rancor and volatile passions that infect the spirit, repair the world by applying the laws fairly and with compassion, learn the lost dialect of love, speak with the gentle voice of poetry and reconciliation – till he drew back, realized his mind had drifted into the deep, unchartable gulf between his own past and the young poet's future, that he hadn' answered her question.

The young poet, unfazed, had another question and still another.

"HOW TO"

books on Wellness proliferate,

how to prevent:
                        Alzheimer's strokes
                        heart disease
                        the big C

how to manage:
                        eating disorders
                        glaucoma
                        menopause
                        stress,

how to treat:
                        the vulnerable hip
                        the frozen shoulder
                        creaky joints
                        incontinence, etc. etc.

There are even manuals on how
                        to resuscitate
                        your fingernails & toes.

Libraries galore, in brief, on how
                        to cheat the End, but

nothing to show you
                        what to live for.

BECOMING A SENIOR

Now that I'm losing my hair and nearing
          the edge,
hear death pecking at my ribs,
certain facts become clear:

I'll never ski to the South Pole,
hang-glide off a glacier,
or become the world's fastest yodeller;

never win the Nobel prize for chemistry,
star in a Hollywood blockbuster
or be a sumo wrestler;

Grand Chess Master, astronaut,
world champion spear thrower,
          I can forget, along with
astrophysics and the Internet;
my time-warped heart's circumscribed, I'll readily
admit, certain things will never fit.

But that's alright, I don't intend
          to grumble or to sulk;
death's an insult on all our plates
and I'd be an ingrate to complain:
after all I'm still alive, loved
and been loved, and while
the mystic rose of contentment eludes
me   still,
I can proclaim: I love my breath,
my sparrow light in this glade of dark.

ELEGY FOR AN AGED QUILTER

As she lay dying that spring morning
on the asphalt amidst
the skeins of chrome & steel, unraveling
in the dark quilt of her spilt blood, a hole
in her chest the size of an apple –
cherry trees beaded the brown earth
with pink glass, doves crooned
in the belfries of nearby steeples.

And when a passerby knelt to clasp
her hand & she opened wide her eyes,
Floral Chains & Friendship Stars,
Warm Hearts & Amish Triangles,
Colonial Ladies & Hummingbirds – all
the Threads of Life – the old familiar ties,
gathered round the The Tree of Life
one last time – A Memory Vest –
to sing & dance.

LOST VOICES

Swept along by
      our onrushing,
kaleidoscopic lives
      there's no time
to swaddle the soul
      with poetry, read
as though the masters
      were still near
waiting in silence
      to make us pause &
reflect, set aglow
      our distracted minds
with radiant words,
      no time – for the slow
turning of pages.

WINTER INVOCATION

Dispersed by swirling winds
snow fell all night;
by morning, the limbs of trees outside
        the sunroom window, sagged
under a thick layer of white.

Wedged like a frozen breath
between memory & absence,
I thought I glimpsed
a gathering of ghosts –
was it a springing cedar bough, a wing,
a shiver of falling snow or just my
imagining? – when I looked again
the ghosts had disappeared,
only the silence remained.

How long Lord, before
you touch my winter mind with
Spring's long, warm, tendrils?

POET'S WISH

Come long awaited
spring, light my cold, dry mind with
your wild green fires.

WINTER GREENING

I'm an old poet winnowed by loss,
often shaken & burdened by the

morning news, the unending daily
rages of the race, with only this

small cache of words to mend my
brokenness, yet some one still thank-

full to be alive, amazed at the misty
radiance of the reborning sun,

clinging however waveringly to the
invisible ladder of prayer, praising

every victory over meanness &
indecency, each poem I write a frail

container of hope waiting to be
opened at dawn.

Epilogue

sound of a wooden pulley
hauling buckets of dawn
from the darkness.

– inspired by Ted Kooser

ABOUT THE AUTHOR

James Clarke is the author of almost twenty books of poetry and memoir, including *Dreamworks, Forced Passage, How to Bribe a Judge, L'Arche Journal, A Mourner's Kaddish, The Raggedy Parade, Silver Mercies,* and *The Way Everyone is Inside.* Many of the poems in this collection have been previously published by Exile Editions, the Legal Studies Forum of the University of Western Virginia law school and Pleasure Boat Studio: A Literary Press , New York city. He is a former Superior Court judge, and his judgments have been published extensively in legal journals. He lives in Guelph, Ontario.

www.ingramcontent.com/pod-product-compliance
Lightning Source LLC
LaVergne TN
LVHW091309080426
835510LV00007B/424